U.K. YEARBOOK

ISBN: 9798621814694

This book gives a fascinating and informative insight into life in the United Kingdom in 1941. It includes everything from the most popular music of the year to the cost of a buying a new house. Additionally, there are chapters covering people in high office, the best-selling films of the year and all the main news and events. Want to know which horse won the Derby or which British personalities were born in 1941? All this and much more awaits you within.

© Liberty Eagle Publishing Ltd. 2020
All Rights Reserved

	Page
Calendar	4
People in High Office	5
British News & Events	9
Worldwide News & Events	20
Births - U.K. Personalities	27
Notable British Deaths	33
Popular Music	35
Top 5 Films	41
Sporting Winners	52
Cost of Living	55
Cartoons	63

FIRST EDITION

People In High Office

Monarch - King George VI
Reign: 11th December 1936 - 6th February 1952
Predecessor: Edward VIII
Successor: Elizabeth II

Prime Minister

Winston Churchill - Conservative
10th May 1940 - 26th July 1945

Ireland

Canada

United States

Taoiseach Of Ireland
Éamon de Valera
Fianna Fáil
29th December 1937
- 18th February 1948

Prime Minister
Mackenzie King
Liberal Party
23rd October 1935
- 15th November 1948

President
Franklin D. Roosevelt
Democratic Party
4th March 1933
- 12th April 1945

 Australia — Prime Minister
Robert Menzies (1939-1941)
Arthur Fadden (1941)
John Curtin (1941-1945)

 Brazil — President
Getúlio Vargas (1930-1945)

 China — Premier
Chiang Kai-shek (1939-1945)

 Cuba — President
Fulgencio Batista (1940-1944)

 Egypt — Prime Minister
Hussein Sirri Pasha (1940-1942)

 France — President
Vacant (1940-1944)

 Germany — Chancellor
Adolf Hitler (1933-1945)

 India — Viceroy of India
Victor Alexander John Hope (1936-1943)

	Italy	Prime Minister Benito Mussolini (1922-1943)
	Japan	Prime Minister Fumimaro Konoe (1940-1941) Hideki Tōjō (1941-1944)
	Mexico	President Manuel Ávila Camacho (1940-1946)
	New Zealand	Prime Minister Peter Fraser (1940-1949)
	Russia	Communist Party Leader Joseph Stalin (1922-1952)
	South Africa	Prime Minister Jan Smuts (1939-1948)
	Spain	Prime Minister Francisco Franco (1938-1973)
	Turkey	Prime Minister Refik Saydam (1939-1942)

BRITISH NEWS & EVENTS

JAN

3rd | Australian and British troops defeat Italian forces at the Battle of Bardia in Libya. The battle takes place between the 3rd and 5th January and is the first British military operation of the Western Desert Campaign of WW2.

9th January: The Avro Manchester Mark III BT308 (a prototype of the Avro Lancaster heavy bomber) is flown by test pilot H. A. 'Sam' Brown on its maiden flight at RAF Ringway in Cheshire. *Interesting facts: The Lancaster Bomber became one of the most heavily used of the Second World War night bombers, delivering 608,612 long tons of bombs during 156,000 sorties. The versatility of the Lancaster was such that it was chosen to equip 617 Squadron and was modified to carry the Upkeep 'Bouncing bomb' designed by Barnes Wallis for Operation Chastise, the attack on German Ruhr valley dams in May 1943. Photo: The prototype Avro Manchester Mark III Reg: BT308 in 1941.*

11th | The British Royal Navy light cruiser HMS Southampton is sunk off Malta after coming under attack from 12 Luftwaffe Stuka dive bombers; 81 men are killed as a result of the attack.

14th | In a BBC radio broadcast from London, Victor de Laveleye asks all Belgians to use the letter V as a rallying sign, being the first letter of victoire (victory) in French and of vrijheid (freedom) in Dutch. This is the beginning of the V campaign and introduces the use of the V sign for victory and freedom.

19th | British troops attack Italian-held Eritrea.

21st | The Daily Worker, the newspaper of the Communist Party of Great Britain, is suppressed by the Labour Home Secretary Herbert Morrison (until September 1942) in view of its continuing pro-Soviet stance.

JAN

21st — Australian and British forces attack and capture the Libyan city of Tobruk from the Italians (21st - 22nd January).

31st — German spy Josef Jakobs parachutes into the village of Ramsey in Cambridgeshire, breaking his ankle in the process. The following morning Jakobs is apprehended by members of the local Home Guard after being notified of his whereabouts by farmers Charles Baldock and Harry Coulson. He was caught still wearing his flying suit and carrying £500 in British currency, forged identity papers, a radio transmitter and a German sausage. *Follow up: Jakobs became last person to be executed at the Tower of London (15th August 1941) after being convicted of espionage under the Treachery Act 1940; he was shot by a military firing squad.*

FEB

5th — The Air Training Corps (ATC) is officially established with King George VI as its Air Commodore-in-Chief. The new ATC's purpose is to provide training programmes to young men who might later join the Royal Air Force.

9th — Winston Churchill makes a speech (broadcast by the BBC) asking the United States to show its support by sending arms to Britain. He ends the speech with an explicit message to President Roosevelt, "Give us the tools, and we will finish the job".

11th — RMS Queen Elizabeth leaves Singapore after a refit and begins her first voyage as a troopship. *Interesting facts: During her war service the Queen Elizabeth carried more than 750,000 troops and sailed some 500,000 miles.*

12th — Terminally ill Police Constable Albert Alexander, a patient at the Radcliffe Infirmary in Oxford, becomes the first person treated with penicillin intravenously. Alexander reacts positively to the drug but due to an insufficient supply he eventually relapses and dies on the 15th March 1941. *Follow up: A successful treatment was achieved 3 months later by Dr Howard Walter Florey and biochemist Ernst Boris Chain. They were responsible for making an effective drug out of penicillin, and alongside Sir Alexander Fleming shared the Nobel Prize in Physiology or Medicine in 1945. It is estimated that their discoveries have to date saved over 200 million lives.*

19th — The start of a three-night Blitz over Swansea, South Wales occurs resulting in 230 deaths and 397 injuries. Swansea's town centre is almost completely obliterated by the 1,273 high explosive bombs and 56,000 Incendiary bombs estimated to have been dropped by the Luftwaffe.

25th — The British submarine HMS Upright torpedoes the Italian cruiser Armando Diaz off the island of Kerkennah on the east coast of Tunisia. The ship takes only six minutes to sink after her magazine blows up; 484 men are killed in the explosion.

MAR

1st — John Gilbert Winant is appointed as United States Ambassador to the United Kingdom in succession to Joseph P. Kennedy; he remains in the post until his resignation in March 1946.

7th — Prime Minister Winston Churchill diverts 58,000 British and Australian troops from Egypt to occupy the Olympus-Vermion line in Greece.

11th	U.S. President Franklin D. Roosevelt signs the Lend-Lease Act into law allowing the country to supply military equipment to Britain (and its foreign allies) whilst still remaining officially neutral.
11th	Luftwaffe air raids on Manchester cause extensive damage to the city. One notable casualty is Old Trafford football stadium, the home of Manchester United F.C., which sees its stands demolished and its pitch wrecked. *Follow up: The stadium was rebuilt after the war and reopened in August 1949. During this time United played at Maine Road, the home of their cross-town rivals Manchester City, at a cost of £5,000 a year plus a percentage of the gate receipts.*

13th March: Clydebank Blitz: Over two nights Clydebank is the target of one of the most intense Luftwaffe bombing raids of World War II. Each night over 200 German bombers attack aiming to destroy naval, shipbuilding and munitions targets. Clydebank's housing bears the brunt of the raids and of its 12,000 homes only 7 properties are left undamaged (4,000 are completely destroyed). The official death toll records 528 casualties; 617 more are seriously injured and 35,000 are made homeless. *Photo: A destroyed tram surrounded by the rubble on Dumbarton Road after the Clydebank Blitz.*

17th	Minister of Labour Ernest Bevin makes a call for women to fill vital jobs in industry and the Auxiliary Services (in December 1941 women begin to be conscripted for war work when Parliament passes the National Service Act).

MAR

27th — Battle of Cape Matapan: Following the interception of Italian signals by the Government Code and Cypher School at Bletchley Park, ships of the Royal Navy and Royal Australian Navy intercept and sink several ships of the Italian Regia Marina off the Peloponnesus coast in the Mediterranean. Over 2,300 Italians lose their lives and 1,015 are taken as prisoners of war in what is Italy's greatest ever defeat at sea.

29th — The first performance of British composer Benjamin Britten's Requiem Symphony takes place at Carnegie Hall, New York.

APR

Birmingham Accident Hospital and Rehabilitation Centre opens as the world's first trauma centre (using the existing buildings of Queen's Hospital in Bath Row, Birmingham).

15th — Two hundred bombers of the Luftwaffe attack military and manufacturing targets in the city of Belfast. Some 900 people die as a result of the bombings and 1,500 are injured (other than London, this is the greatest loss of life in any night raid during the Blitz).

19th April: The heaviest air-raids of the year take place on London; 1,000 tons of high explosive and 153,000 incendiaries are dropped killing 1,200 people. *Facts: London was targeted a total of 71 times by the Luftwaffe's bombing campaign during the Blitz. During these raids 32,000 civilians in London were killed and 87,000 seriously injured.*

APR

21st — After the surrender of the Greek forces in Albania to the Germans the previous day, the final decision for the evacuation of Commonwealth forces from Greece, to Crete and Egypt, is taken.

22nd — The Portland Square air raid shelter in Plymouth is struck during bombing; 76 people are killed, the greatest civilian loss of life in the Plymouth Blitz.

26th — The Official recipe for Woolton Pie is reported in The Times. The pie is the invention of Francis Latry, the head chef at the Savoy Hotel in London, and is named after the Minister of Food, Lord Woolton. *Fun fact: The pie contained no meat and was one of many recipes introduced to the British people by the Ministry of Food to ensure that a nutritional diet could be maintained despite food shortages.*

MAY

1st — A seven-night bombardment by the Luftwaffe on Liverpool, the largest port on the west coast and being of significant importance to the British war effort, devastates the city. *Follow up: The sustained heavy bombing on Merseyside during the 'May Blitz' was carried out by 681 bombers and put 69 out of 144 cargo berths out of action. The raids demolished 4,400 homes in Liverpool and damaged a further 61,900; over 75,000 people on Merseyside were left homeless. By the end of the seven nights 1453 people had been killed in Liverpool, 257 in Bootle, 28 in Birkenhead and 3 in Wallasey.*

2nd — British combat operations against the rebel government of Rashid Ali, who had seized power with assistance from Germany and Italy, begin in the Kingdom of Iraq. *Follow up: The campaign results in the downfall of Ali's government on the 31st May 1941, the re-occupation of Iraq, and the return to power of the Regent of Iraq, Prince 'Abd al-Ilah, an ally to the United Kingdom.*

6th — Greenock in Scotland is intensively bombed by the Luftwaffe who target the shipyards and berthed ships around the town. Over two nights 271 people are killed and over 10,200 injured. From a total of 180,000 homes nearly 25,000 suffer damage and 5,000 are destroyed outright.

9th — The German submarine U-110 is captured by the Royal Navy in the North Atlantic after being forced to surface by depth charges. On board is the latest Enigma cryptography machine (and the U-boat's code books) which Allied cryptographers later use to break coded German messages.

10th — The House of Commons is damaged by incendiary bombs dropped by the Luftwaffe; the Commons Chamber is entirely destroyed by fire.

10th — London's Queen's Hall, the venue for The Proms, is bombed by the Luftwaffe. The concert series relocates to the Royal Albert Hall (which today remains their principal venue).

10th — Rudolf Hess parachutes into Scotland at Floors Farm, Eaglesham, south of Glasgow. He is discovered still struggling with his parachute by local ploughman David McLean who contacts the local Home Guard unit. They escort their captive to their headquarters in Busby, East Renfrewshire. Hess says he has an important message for the Duke of Hamilton and claims to be on a peace mission.

15th — The first British jet-engined aircraft, the prototype Gloster E.28/39 (also referred to as the Gloster Whittle or Gloster Pioneer) is flown for the first time at RAF Cranwell in Lincolnshire by Flight Lieutenant Gerry Sayer.

MAY

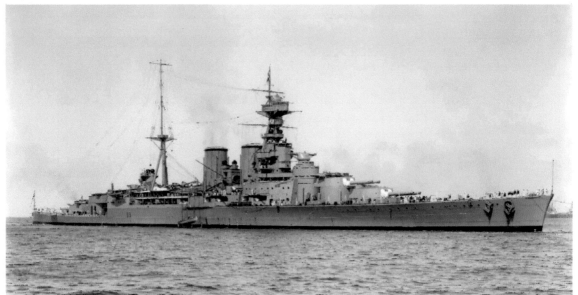

24th May: In the Battle of the Denmark Strait the German battleship Bismarck sinks the pride of the Royal Navy, the battlecruiser HMS Hood. Hood was struck near her aft ammunition magazines, and sank within 3 minutes with the loss of all but 3 of the 1418 men aboard. *Photo: HMS Hood (1924) - the last battlecruiser built for the Royal Navy.*

24th	Off the coast of Sicily, the British submarine HMS Upholder torpedoes and sinks the Italian ocean liner turned troopship SS Conte Rosso. Of the 2,729 soldiers and crew aboard, 1,300 were killed.
27th	In the Atlantic, approximately 350 miles west of Brest, France, a severely damaged Bismarck, which had been relentlessly pursued by the Royal Navy since the sinking of HMS Hood, is scuttled with heavy loss of life. Out of a crew of over 2,200 men only 114 survived (British warships rescued 111 of the survivors from Bismarck).

JUN

1st	Arthur 'Bomber' Harris is promoted to the acting rank of air marshal. *Follow up: Harris would eventually go on to become the Marshal of the Royal Air Force (1st January 1946), the highest rank in the British Royal Air Force.*
1st	Oliver Lyttleton, President of the Board of Trade, announces the introduction of clothes rationing. The news comes as a complete surprise to most people but was needed to reduce production and consumption of civilian clothes, and to safeguard raw materials and release workers (and factory space) for war production. *Further information: Clothes rationing went on until the 15th March 1949 during which time people were urged to "Make do and mend". Everyone received a Clothing Book with 60 coupons (children were allocated an extra 10 coupons) which allowed them to buy one completely new set of clothes a year.*
8th	The British and Free French forces invade Syria and Lebanon.
22nd	Operation Barbarossa: Nazi Germany and its allies invades the Soviet Union. Winston Churchill promises all possible British assistance to the Soviet Union in a worldwide broadcast: "Any man or state who fights against Nazidom will have our aid. Any man or state who marches with Hitler is our foe."

JUL

	The British Army's Special Air Service is formed by David Stirling (originally called "L" Detachment, Special Air Service Brigade).
2nd	Noël Coward's comic play Blithe Spirit premieres at the Piccadilly Theatre in the West End of London. *Fun fact: The play's run of 1,997 consecutive performances set a record for a non-musical play in the West End (the run was eventually surpassed by Agatha Christie's The Mousetrap in 1957).*
5th	The British troopship SS Anselm is torpedoed and sunk by the German submarine U-96 in the Atlantic Ocean; 250 of the 1,310 on men onboard were lost.
7th	Neutral American forces take over the defence of Iceland from the British.
12th	The Anglo-Soviet Agreement is signed by the United Kingdom and the Soviet Union against Germany. Both powers pledge to assist each other and not make separate peace with Germany.
15th	The MAUD Report (edited by James Chadwick) is approved and concludes an atomic bomb is feasible. *Follow up: The report was presented by Vannevar Bush to President Roosevelt in October 1941 and inspired the U.S. government to pour millions of dollars into the pursuit of an atomic bomb.*

19th July: Winston Churchill launches his "V for Victory" campaign buoyed by the success of Victor de Laveleye's call (on the 14th January) for the use the letter V as a rallying sign. The BBC also sets out a plan for the campaign and puts assistant news editor Douglas Ritchie, posing as "Colonel Britton", in charge.

23rd	An Italian Savoia-Marchetti SM.79 bomber aircraft torpedoes and damages the British destroyer HMS Fearless (the detonation kills 27 and wounds 11 of the crew). Fearless cannot be saved and is sunk 58 miles north of Bône, Algeria.

AUG

	The Political Warfare Executive is formed to disseminate information to Germany and its occupied countries.
9th	Winston Churchill, onboard HMS Prince of Wales, reaches Naval Station Argentia in Newfoundland for talks with President Roosevelt. The Atlantic Charter, setting out American and British goals for the period following the end of World War II, is agreed as a result.

9th August: RAF pilot Douglas Bader, on an offensive patrol over the French coast, is forced to bale out after a mid-air collision and is taken prisoner by the Germans. *Follow up: Despite having lost both his legs in a flying accident in 1931, Bader made a number of escape attempts and was eventually sent to the prisoner of war camp at Colditz Castle. He remained there until April 1945 when the camp was liberated by the First United States Army. Photo: Highly decorated RAF flying ace Douglas Bader (credited with 22 aerial victories and 4 shared victories).*

16th	HMS Mercury Royal Navy Signals School and Combined Signals School opens at Leydene House near Petersfield in Hampshire.
18th	The National Fire Service (NFS) is established by the amalgamation of the wartime national Auxiliary Fire Service (AFS) and the local authority fire brigades (about 1,600 of them). *Interesting facts: The NFS existed until 1948 and at peak strength had 370,000 personnel including 80,000 women.*
25th	The Anglo-Soviet invasion of Iran (Operation Countenance), to secure Iranian oil fields and ensure Allied supply lines for the USSR, begins.
30th	The German troopships SS Bahia Laura and SS Donau are sunk by the British submarine HMS Trident of Seloen Island, Norway; 1,700 German troops are lost on the two ships.

AUG

30th	The first official 'Shetland Bus' clandestine mission, using Norwegian fishing boats between Shetland and German-occupied Norway, departs for Bergen from Hamnavoe, on the west side of Lunna Ness. Officially named the Norwegian Naval Independent Unit (NNIU), the Shetland Bus crossings would continue until the surrender of Nazi Germany on the 8th May 1945.
30th	Winston Churchill becomes the first national leader to approve a nuclear weapons programme (codename Tube Alloys).
30th	A German Lorenz cipher machine operator sends a 4,000-character message twice, from Athens to Vienna, without changing the key settings. This allows British mathematician Bill Tutte to decipher the machine's coding mechanism and becomes an important source of "Ultra" intelligence, contributing significantly to the eventual Allied victory against Germany.

SEP

17th	Rezā Shāh of Iran is forced to resign in favour of his son Mohammad Reza Pahlavi, under pressure from the United Kingdom and the Soviet Union, concluding the Anglo-Soviet invasion of Iran.
29th	The first Moscow Conference begins; U.S. representative Averell Harriman and British representative Lord Beaverbrook meet with Soviet foreign minister Vyacheslav Molotov to arrange urgent assistance for Russia.

OCT

The first Ronald Searle cartoon to feature St Trinian's School is published in the magazine Lilliput. *Interesting facts: Searle, who had been posted to Malaya with the 18th Infantry Division, had been unaware he had been published until February 1942 when he picked up an abandoned copy of Lilliput in a Singapore side street. Captured by the Japanese he became a POW in Changi Prison and in the Kwai jungle. Photos: Ronald Serle (1956) and a copy of his first St Trinian's cartoon for Lilliput.*

OCT

- 1st — U.S. President Franklin D. Roosevelt approves US$1bn in Lend-Lease aid to Britain.
  The New Zealand Division of the Royal Navy becomes the Royal New Zealand Navy.
- 31st — A fire at the H. Booth & Son clothing factory in Huddersfield kills 49, most of them women and young girls. The fire is caused by a smoker's pipe left alight inside a raincoat pocket.

NOV

- 1st — Politician Sir Charles Trevelyan announces that he is donating his family home, Wallington Hall, Northumberland, to the National Trust. Complete with the estate and farms, it is the first donation of its kind to the National Trust.
- 10th — In a speech at the Mansion House in London, Winston Churchill promises "should the United States become involved in war with Japan, the British declaration will follow within the hour."

13th November: The Royal Navy aircraft carrier HMS Ark Royal is hit by the German submarine U-81 off Gibraltar; she capsizes and sinks under tow the next day. *Photo: A listing Ark Royal hands survivors over to HMS Legion before sinking; of her crew of 1,488 there was just one fatality, Able Seaman Edward Mitchell.*

- 18th — Operation Crusader, a British Eighth Army operation to relieve the Siege of Tobruk in North Africa, begins. *Follow up: Tobruk is relieved by the Eighth Army on the 27th November.*
- 22nd — HMS Devonshire sinks the commerce raiding German auxiliary cruiser Atlantis. *Atlantis facts: During its WW2 campaign the cruiser sank or captured 22 ships (13 British), and travelled more 100,000 miles in 602 days.*

DEC

5th	Britain declares war on Finland, Hungary and Romania.
6th	The British submarine HMS Perseus strikes an Italian mine off Cephalonia, 7 miles north of Zakynthos in the Ionian Sea; 31-year-old leading stoker John Capes is the only survivor out of the 61 men on board. *Notes: After escaping from the submarine Capes swam 5 miles to the island of Cephalonia where he was hidden by islanders for 18 months before being smuggled to Smyrna, Turkey. He was subsequently awarded a British Empire Medal.*
8th	A declaration of war by the Empire of Japan on the United States and the British Empire is published on the front page of all Japanese newspapers' evening editions. The declaration appears an hour after Japanese forces had begun their attacks on the U.S. naval base at Pearl Harbor and on British forces in Malaya, Singapore, and Hong Kong.
10th	The Royal Navy ships HMS Prince of Wales and HMS Repulse are sunk by Japanese aircraft near Kuantan, in the South China Sea. They are the first capital ships to be sunk solely by air power on the open sea.
13th	Britain, New Zealand, and South Africa declare war on Bulgaria.
14th	The German submarine U-557 torpedoes and sinks the British light cruiser Galatea off Alexandria, Egypt. Galatea's Captain E.W.B. Sim, 22 officers and 447 ratings are killed; some 100 survivors are picked up by the destroyers Griffin and Hotspur.
18th	Parliament passes the second National Service Act widening the scope of conscription still further. All unmarried women and childless widows between the ages of 20 and 30 are liable to be called-up, and men are now required to do some form of National Service up to the age of 60, including military service for those under 51.
19th	Italian Regia Marina divers on human torpedoes place limpet mines on the Royal Navy Mediterranean Fleet in port at Alexandria, Egypt. The battleships Queen Elizabeth and Valiant are severely damaged in the raid.
22nd	The Arcadia Conference opens in Washington, D.C., the first meeting on military strategy between the heads of government of the United Kingdom and the United States following the latter's entry into the war.
25th	The Battle of Hong Kong ends after 17 days with surrender, by Governor Sir Mark Aitchison Young, of the Crown colony of Hong Kong to the Japanese.
25th	Field Marshal Sir Alan Brooke succeeds Field Marshal Sir John Dill as Chief of the Imperial General Staff, an office he will hold until the 25th June 1946.
27th	Winston Churchill becomes the first British Prime Minister to address a Joint session of the U.S. Congress. He ends his speech, which runs for over 30 minutes, to thunderous applause. He then flashes a V for victory sign before leaving the chamber. The New York Times describes his address as "full of bubbling humour, biting denunciation of totalitarian enemies, stern courage - and hard facts".

60 WORLDWIDE NEWS & EVENTS

1. 1st January: Thailand's Prime Minister Plaek Phibunsongkhram decrees that the 1st January will now be the official start of the new year. *Note: Songkran was the official new year until 1888, after which it was switched to the 1st April.*

2. 4th January: The Merrie Melodies cartoon Elmer's Pet Rabbit is released and is the first to use Bugs Bunny's name on-screen. *Fun facts: Bugs Bunny's official debut was in A Wild Hare (1940), but the prototypical version of Bugs Bunny appeared in four cartoons before this dating back to Happy Rabbit in Porky's Hare Hunt (1938). Bugs Bunny has appeared in more films than any other cartoon character and has his own star on the Hollywood Walk of Fame. Pictured: Bugs Bunny's evolution from Happy Rabbit in 1938 to the present day.*

3. 6th January: In an address known as the Four Freedoms speech (technically the 1941 State of the Union address), President Roosevelt proposes four fundamental freedoms that people everywhere in the world ought to enjoy; 1. Freedom of speech, 2. Freedom of worship, 3. Freedom from want, 4. Freedom from fear.

4. 14th January: Commerce raiding German auxiliary cruiser Pinguin captures the Norwegian whaling fleet near Bouvet Island, effectively ending Southern Ocean whaling for the duration of the war. *Notes: Pinguin's operation against the Norwegian whaling fleet was the single most successful performance by a German auxiliary cruiser in World War II. More than 36,000 tons of shipping, a supply-ship, two factory ships, 11 whalers, 20,000 tons of whale oil with a value of over $4 million, and 10,000 tons of fuel oil were captured.*

5. 31st January: Boxer Joe Louis knocks out Red Burman in 5 rounds to retain The Ring and lineal heavyweight titles. This is the 13th defence of his titles since winning them from James J. Braddock on the 22nd June 1937, and he goes on to defend them a further 6 times in 1941 against; Gus Dorazio, Abe Simon, Tony Musto, Buddy Baer, Billy Conn, and Lou Nova. *Fun facts: In all, Louis made 25 defences of his heavyweight titles between 1937 and 1948, and was a world champion for 11 years and 10 months. His most remarkable record is that he knocked out 23 opponents in 27 title fights, including five world champions.*

6. 6th February: Lieutenant-General Erwin Rommel is appointed commander of the Afrika Korps (the German expeditionary force in Africa).

7.	23rd February: The chemical element 94, plutonium, is first synthesised by Glenn T. Seaborg, Arthur C. Wahl, Joseph W. Kennedy and Edwin McMillan at the University of California, Berkeley; it is kept secret until after the atomic bombings of Hiroshima and Nagasaki.
8.	25th February: A general strike in the German-occupied Netherlands begins in defence of persecuted Dutch Jews, and against the anti-Jewish measures and activities of the Nazis in general. *Notes: The 1941 February Strike is considered to be the first public protest against the Nazis in occupied Europe, and the only mass protest against the deportation of Jews to be organised by non-Jews.*
9.	27th February: The 13th Academy Awards, honouring the best in film in 1940, are held at the Biltmore Hotel in Los Angeles, California. The winners include Alfred Hitchcock's film Rebecca (his only film to win Best Picture), James Stewart and Ginger Rogers. Disney's Pinocchio becomes the first animated film to take home a competitive Oscar, winning for both Best Original Score and Best Original Song. *Notes: This is the first year that sealed envelopes are used to keep secret the names of the winners, leading to the famous phrase: "May I have the envelope, please?" The accounting firm of Price Waterhouse is hired to count the ballots after the fiasco of leaked voting results in 1939 by the Los Angeles Times.*
10.	March: Captain America and his sidekick Bucky make their first appearance in Captain America Comics No.1, from Timely Comics, a predecessor of Marvel Comics (although cover-dated March 1941, it actually went on sale the 20th December 1940). *Fun facts: The first issue, showing the protagonist punching Nazi leader Adolf Hitler, went on to sell nearly one million copies. In August 2011 a copy of the comic (graded 9.2) sold for $343,057.*

11. 22nd March: James Stewart is inducted into the U.S. Army and becomes the first major American movie star to wear a military uniform in World War II. *Follow up: Stewart served as a pilot during World War II and was awarded two Distinguished Flying Crosses and four Air Medals. He later went on to serve in the Vietnam War, rising to the rank of brigadier general in the U.S. Air Force Reserve. Photos: Corporal Stewart is commissioned a Second Lieutenant in the U.S. Army Air Corps at Moffett Field, California (1942) / Brigadier General James Stewart (1968).*

12.	April: The Valley of Geysers is discovered on Russia's Kamchatka Peninsula by Soviet geologist Tatyana Ustinova.
13.	6th April: Germany invades the Kingdom of Yugoslavia and Greece.
14.	13th April: The Soviet-Japanese Neutrality Pact is signed in Moscow.

15.	18th April: Greek Prime Minister Alexandros Koryzis commits suicide as German troops approach Athens.
16.	1st May: Orson Welles' film Citizen Kane premieres at the Palace Theatre in New York City. Starring himself, Joseph Cotten and Dorothy Corningore, the picture is Welles's first feature film.
17.	1st May: The breakfast cereal CheeriOats is introduced by American manufacturer General Mills; the cereal is renamed Cheerios in 1945.
18.	5th May: Emperor Haile Selassie enters Addis Ababa after it has been liberated from Italian forces; this date is subsequently commemorated as Liberation Day in Ethiopia.
19.	5th May: French couturier Gabrielle 'Coco' Chanel releases her first perfume, Chanel No.5.
20.	6th May: Joseph Stalin replaces Vyacheslav Molotov to become the Premier of the Soviet Union.
21.	7th May: Glenn Miller records the big band / swing tune Chattanooga Choo Choo for RCA Victor. Written by Mack Gordon and composed by Harry Warren, it features in the 1941 movie Sun Valley Serenade, and becomes the first song to receive a gold record with sales of 1.2 million copies.
22.	12th May: Konrad Zuse presents the Z3 to an audience of scientists in Berlin. It is the world's first working programmable, fully automatic computer.
23.	12th May: Martin Bormann succeeds Rudolf Hess as Adolf Hitler's deputy.
24.	25th May: 5,000 people drown in a storm in the Ganges Delta region of India.
25.	1st June: The Battle of Crete ends as Crete surrenders to invading German forces.
26.	5th June: Around 4,000 Chongqing residents are asphyxiated in a tunnel during the bombing of Chongqing, China, by the Japanese.
27.	18th June: The German-Turkish Treaty of Friendship is signed between Nazi Germany and Turkey, in Ankara.
28.	25th June: Finland (as a co-belligerent with Germany) attacks the Soviet Union to start the Continuation War.
29.	28th June: The U.S. Office of Scientific Research and Development is created with Vannevar Bush as its director. It is charged with research into a wide variety of projects, one of which would be the secret S-1 Section whose work into the development the first atomic weapons provided the groundwork for the Manhattan Project.
30.	30th June: The massacres (pogroms) of thousands of Jews by Ukrainian nationalists, Nazi SS paramilitary death squads (Einsatzgruppen), and local crowds, begin in the city of Lwów (now Lviv, Ukraine).
31.	5th July: A border war, known locally as the War of '41, begins between Peru and Ecuador; a ceasefire agreement between the two countries is reached on the 31st July 1941.
32.	19th July: The MGM cartoon, The Midnight Snack, by William Hanna and Joseph Barbera, is released and features the second appearance of Tom and Jerry. *Fun facts: It is the first cartoon in which the duo are officially named. They had previously appeared in Puss Gets the Boot (1940), but had been called Jasper (Tom) and Jinx (Jerry).*
33.	31st July: The Holocaust: Under instructions from Adolf Hitler, Nazi official Hermann Göring orders S.S. General Reinhard Heydrich to work out the plan of the Final Solution of the Jewish Problem (i.e. the deliberate and systematic extermination of all Jewish people).
34.	6th August: Six-year-old Elaine Esposito undergoes an appendectomy and lapses into a coma that lasts for a record-breaking 37 years; Edwarda O'Bara and Aruna Shanbaug later exceeded Esposito's record, both spent 42 years in a coma.

35.	21st August: In revenge for the execution two days earlier of French Resistance member Samuel Tyszelman, communist activist Pierre Georges (and three companions) shoot German soldier Alfons Moser in occupied Paris; Moser's death initiates a cycle of assassinations and retribution that results in 500 French hostages being executed over the following months.
36.	28th August: German troops capture Tallinn, Estonia from the Soviet Union. Attacks on the evacuating Soviet ships leave more than 12,400 dead in one of the bloodiest naval battles of the war.
37.	29th August: Robert Menzies resigns as Prime Minister of Australia after losing the support of his party. Arthur Fadden, leader of the Country Party, consequently becomes Prime Minister, while former Prime Minister Billy Hughes replaces Menzies as UAP leader. *Follow up: Menzies subsequently helps to create the new Liberal Party and is elected its inaugural leader in August 1945. At the 1949 federal election he leads the Liberal-Country coalition to victory and returns as prime minister, a position he holds until the 26th January 1966.*

38. 1st September: The Messerschmitt Me 163 Komet, a German rocket-powered interceptor aircraft designed by Alexander Lippisch, is flown for the first time. *Interesting facts: The Komet is the only rocket-powered fighter aircraft ever to have been operational and is the first piloted aircraft of any type to exceed 1000 km/h (621 mph) in level flight. Photo: A Messerschmitt Me163b, circa 1944.*

39.	1st September: A decree issued and signed by German SS officer Reinhard Heydrich requires all Jews over the age of six, in the Reich and the Protectorate of Bohemia and Moravia, to wear a yellow Star of David with the word Jude (German for Jew) inscribed within it on their outer clothing. The practice is gradually introduced in other German-occupied areas using local words (e.g., Juif in France, Jood in the Netherlands).

40.	8th September: A siege of the Soviet city of Leningrad (now Saint Petersburg) by German troops begins. *Notes: The Siege of Leningrad was one of the deadliest and most destructive sieges in the history of the world. It would last for 872 days and would lead to more than 2,000,000 Soviet civilian and military casualties, as well as 580,000 German casualties.*
41.	11th September: Construction of the Pentagon (the headquarters of the U.S. Department of Defense) begins in Arlington County, Virginia. Designed by architect George Bergstrom, the Pentagon is officially opened on the 14th January 1943 (although the buildings first employees moved in on the 30th April 1942). *Interesting facts: The Pentagon is the world's largest office building with about 600,000m² of space, and has 23,000 military and civilian employees, and another 3,000 non-defence support personnel.*
42.	27th September: The National Liberation Front (Greece) (the main Greek Resistance movement) is established, and Georgios Siantos is appointed its first acting leader.

43. 27th September: The first Liberty ship, the SS Patrick Henry, is launched from the U.S. city of Baltimore, Maryland. *Interesting facts: Liberty ships were a class of cargo ship that was developed to meet British orders for transports to replace ships that had been lost. American shipyards built 2,710 Liberty ships between 1941 and 1945, the largest number of ships ever produced to a single design. Photo: The Patrick Henry being launched at the Bethlehem-Fairfield Shipyard in Baltimore.*

44. 29th-30th September: German forces, under the command of SS-Standartenführer Paul Blobel, massacre 33,771 Jews at Babi Yar in the Ukrainian capital Kiev.
45. 2nd October: Operation Typhoon begins as Germany launches an all-out offensive against Moscow.
46. 7th October: John Curtin becomes the 14th Prime Minister of Australia following the defeat of Arthur Fadden's Country / UAP Coalition Government.
47. 17th October: General Hideki Tōjō becomes the 40th Prime Minister of Japan.
48. 22nd-24th October: Romanian soldiers, German Einsatzgruppe SS and local ethnic Germans massacre some 25,000 to 34,000 Jews in the city of Odessa in Ukraine.

49. 31st October: After 14 years, work ceases on sculpting Mount Rushmore National Memorial in the U.S. town of Keystone, South Dakota. *Fun facts: Sculpted by Gutzon Borglum and 400 workers, the colossal 60-foot-high carvings of Presidents George Washington, Thomas Jefferson, Theodore Roosevelt, and Abraham Lincoln were carved to represent the first 130 years of American history. Today Mount Rushmore is South Dakota's top tourist attraction bringing in around three million tourists every year from all over the world.*

50. 7th November: Soviet leader Joseph Stalin delivers an historic address in which he claims that, in 4 months of war, Germany has lost 4.5 million soldiers (a gross exaggeration), and that a Soviet victory is near.
51. 7th November: The Soviet hospital ship Armenia is sunk by German aircraft while evacuating civilians and wounded soldiers from Crimea; it has been estimated that approximately 5,000 to 7,000 people were killed during the sinking, making it one of the deadliest maritime disasters in history. There were only 8 survivors.
52. 19th November: A battle between the Australian cruiser HMAS Sydney and German auxiliary cruiser Kormoran takes place off the coast of Western Australia. The Sydney sinks with the loss of all hands (645), and the Kormoran is scuttled due to damage sustained during the battle; 318 of the 399 crew aboard the German ship are rescued and placed in prisoner of war camps for the duration of World War II.
53. 26th November: A task force of 6 aircraft carriers, commanded by Japanese Vice Admiral Chūichi Nagumo, leaves Hitokapu Bay for Pearl Harbor, under strict radio silence.

| 54. | 30th November and 8th December: Nazi Einsatzgruppe SS, with the help of local collaborators, kill 25,000 Jews in or on the way to Rumbula forest near Riga, Latvia. |
| 55. | December: Wonder Woman makes her first appearance in All Star Comics No.8 (the comic was actually released in October 1941 but was cover dated December 1941 / January 1942). |

56. 7th December: The Imperial Japanese Navy launch a surprise, pre-emptive military strike on the U.S. Navy fleet at Pearl Harbor. The base is attacked by 353 Imperial Japanese aircraft launched in two waves from its six aircraft carriers. *Casualties and losses: As a result of the attack all eight Navy battleships at Pearl Harbor are damaged, with four sunk. The Japanese also damage a number of other ships including 3 cruisers and 3 destroyers. Additionally, 188 U.S. aircraft are destroyed and 159 damaged; 2,403 Americans are killed during the attack. Japanese losses include 29 aircraft and five midget submarines; 64 Japanese servicemen are killed and one is captured. Photo: USS Arizona on fire after the Imperial Japanese Navy Air Service attack on Pearl Harbor, December 7, 1941; she sank, with the loss of 1,177 officers and crewmen.*

57.	8th December: President Roosevelt delivers his famous "Infamy Speech", and within an hour Congress passes a formal declaration of war against Japan.
58.	11th December: Japan's allies, Germany and Italy, declare war on the United States; the U.S. responds in kind.
59.	13th December: Sweden's lowest ever temperature of -53°C is recorded in the village of Malgovik, Lappland.
60.	24th December: The Dutch submarine HNLMS K XVI becomes the first Allied submarine to sink a Japanese warship after it torpedoes the Japanese destroyer Sagiri. The following day HNLMS K XVI is itself torpedoed by the Japanese submarine I-66 (later renumbered to be I-166) off Borneo; all 36 aboard are killed.

Births
British Personalities
Born in 1941

Graham Chapman
b. 8th January 1941
d. 4th October 1989
Comedian, writer, actor, author and member of comedy group Monty Python.

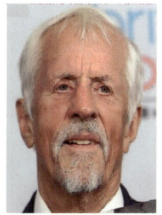

Michael Apted, CMG
b. 10th February 1941

Director, producer, writer and actor.

Paddy Ashdown, GCMG, CH, KBE, PC
b. 27th February 1941
d. 22nd December 2018
Politician and diplomat who served as Leader of the Liberal Democrats.

Bill Tarmey
b. 4th April 1941
d. 9th November 2012
Actor, singer and author known for playing Jack Duckworth in Coronation Street.

Gordon Kaye
b. 7th April 1941
d. 23rd January 2017
Actor and singer best known for playing
René Artois in 'Allo 'Allo!

Cornelia Frances, OAM
b. 7th April 1941
d. 28th May 2018
British-Australian actress.

Vivienne Westwood, DBE, RDI
b. 8th April 1941

Fashion designer and businesswoman.

Bobby Moore, OBE
b. 12th April 1941
d. 24th February 1993
Footballer who was captain of the England
team that won the 1966 FIFA World Cup.

Ed 'Stewpot' Stewart
b. 23rd April 1941
d. 9th January 2016
Broadcaster known for his work as a DJ on
BBC Radio and as a presenter on BBC TV.

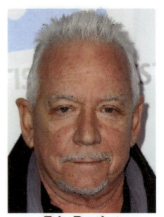

Eric Burdon
b. 11th May 1941

Singer-songwriter and actor who sang with
the rock band the Animals.

Joe Brown, MBE
b. 13th May 1941

Entertainer who has worked as a singer and guitarist for more than six decades.

Miriam Margolyes, OBE
b. 18th May 1941

British-Australian actress and voice artist.

Ming Campbell, CH, CBE, PC, QC, Kt
b. 22nd May 1941

Politician, advocate and former athlete who served as Leader of the Liberal Democrats.

Charlie Watts
b. 2nd June 1941

Drummer with Rolling Stones since 1963.

Mike Yarwood, OBE
b. 14th June 1941

Impressionist, comedian and actor.

Delia Smith, CH, CBE
b. 18th June 1941

Celebrity chef and television presenter.

Michael Howard, CH, PC, QC
b. 7th July 1941

Politician who served as Leader of the Conservative Party.

Bill Oddie, OBE
b. 7th July 1941

Writer, comedian, musician, artist, birder, conservationist, TV presenter and actor.

Craig Douglas
b. 12th August 1941

Pop singer whose career was at its greatest during the late 1950s and early 1960s.

John McNally
b. 30th August 1941

Guitarist and vocalist who was one of the original founders of The Searchers in 1957.

Sue MacGregor, CBE
b. 30th August 1941

Broadcaster best known for presenting Woman's Hour and the Today programme.

Martine Beswick
b. 26th September 1941

Actress, model and former Bond girl.

Stephanie Cole, OBE
b. 5th October 1941

Stage, television, radio and film actress.

John Snow
b. 13th October 1941

Cricketer who played for Sussex and England.

Hank Marvin
b. 28th October 1941

Vocalist and songwriter best known as the lead guitarist of the Shadows.

John Pullin
b. 1st November 1941

International rugby union player.

Bruce Welch, OBE
b. 2nd November 1941

Guitarist, songwriter, producer and singer best known as a member of the Shadows.

Tom Conti
b. 22nd November 1941

Actor, theatre director and novelist.

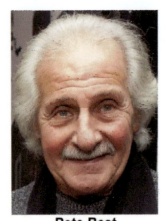

Pete Best
b. 24th November 1941

Musician and former drummer with the Beatles.

Sir Geoff Hurst, MBE
b. 8th December 1941

Footballer who scored a hat-trick in the 1966 World Cup final.

Prince William of Gloucester
b. 18th December 1941
d. 28th August 1972
Grandson of King George V who at birth was fourth in line to the throne.

Ray Thomas
b. 29th December 1941
d. 4th January 2018
Musician, flautist, singer and founding member / composer of the Moody Blues.

Sarah Miles
b. 31st December 1941

Theatre and film actress.

Sir Alex Ferguson, CBE
b. 31st December 1941

Football manager and player noted for his time managing Manchester United.

Notable British Deaths

Amy Johnson, CBE (b. 1st July 1903; disappeared presumed dead 5th January 1941) - Pioneering English pilot who in May 1930 became the first woman to fly solo from England to Australia. Flying solo, or with her Scottish husband Jim Mollison, she set many long-distance records around the globe during the 1930s.

8th Jan	Lieutenant General Robert Stephenson Smyth Baden-Powell, 1st Baron Baden-Powell, OM, GCMG, GCVO, KCB, KStJ, DL (b. 22nd February 1857) - British Army officer, writer, founder and first Chief Scout of the world-wide Boy Scout Movement.
10th Jan	Frank Bridge (b. 26th February 1879) - Composer, violist and conductor.
12th Feb	Charles Francis Annesley Voysey (b. 28th May 1857) - Architect and furniture and textile designer.
11th Mar	Sir Henry Walford Davies, KCVO, OBE (b. 6th September 1869) - Composer, organist, conductor and educator who held the title Master of the King's Music from 1934 until 1941.
28th Mar	Adeline Virginia Woolf (b. 25th January 1882) - Writer considered one of the most important modernist 20th century authors.
5th Apr	Sir Herbert Nigel Gresley, CBE (b. 19th June 1876) - One of Britain's most famous steam locomotive engineers who rose to become Chief Mechanical Engineer of the London and North Eastern Railway.
16th Apr	Josiah Charles Stamp, 1st Baron Stamp, GCB, GBE, FBA (b. 21st June 1880) - Industrialist, economist, civil servant, statistician and writer who served as both a director of the Bank of England and chairman of the London, Midland and Scottish Railway.
17th Apr	Albert Allick Bowlly (b. 7th January 1898) - Mozambican-born, South African / British vocalist and jazz guitarist who recorded more than 1,000 songs.
7th May	Sir James George Frazer, OM, FRS, FRSE, FBA (b. 1st January 1854) - Social anthropologist and folklorist influential in the early stages of the modern studies of mythology and comparative religion.
23rd May	Herbert Austin, 1st Baron Austin, KBE (b. 8th November 1866) - Automobile designer and builder who founded the Austin Motor Company.

24th May	Vice Admiral Lancelot Ernest Holland, CB (b. 13th September 1887) - Royal Navy officer who commanded the British force in the Battle of the Denmark Strait; he was lost alongside 1414 other men when HMS Hood was sunk by the German battleship Bismarck.
1st Jun	Sir Hugh Seymour Walpole, CBE (b. 13th March 1884) - Novelist and best-selling author during the 1920s and 1930s.
15th Jun	Evelyn Underhill (b. 6th December 1875) - Anglo-Catholic writer and pacifist known for her numerous works on religion and spiritual practice.
11th Jul	Sir Arthur John Evans, FRS, FBA, FREng (b. 8th July 1851) - Archaeologist and pioneer in the study of Aegean civilization in the Bronze Age. Evans is most famous for unearthing the palace of Knossos on the Greek island of Crete.
29th Jul	James Albert Stephenson (b. 14th April 1889) - Stage and film actor.
12th Aug	Robert Peel (b. 12th February 1857) - Cricketer who played for Yorkshire and represented England in 20 Test matches.

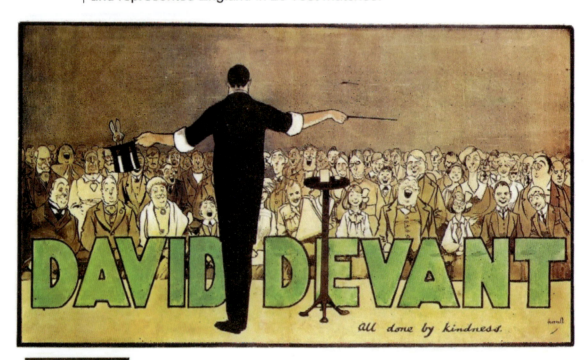

 David Devant (b. 22nd February 1868 - d. 13th October 1941) - Magician, shadowgraphist and film exhibitor who was the first President of The Magic Circle. Devant is regarded by magicians as a consummate exponent of suave and witty presentation of stage illusion. Magic historian Jim Steinmeyer describes him as "England's greatest magician and arguably the greatest magician of the 20th century".

20th Oct	Kenneth Farnes (b. 8th July 1911) - Cricketer and RAF Volunteer Reserve pilot. Farnes played in 15 Tests matches for England between 1934 and 1939.
7th Nov	Frank Pick, Hon. RIBA (b. 23rd November 1878) - Transport administrator who was the chief executive officer and vice-chairman of the London Passenger Transport Board from its creation in 1933 until 1940.
7th Dec	Cecil Forsyth (b. 30th November 1870) - Composer and musicologist.

POPULAR MUSIC

Glenn Miller & His Orchestra	No.1	Chattanooga Choo Choo
The Ink Spots	No.2	We Three (My Echo, My Shadow & Me)
Jimmy Dorsey	No.3	Maria Elena
Bing Crosby	No.4	Dolores
The Ink Spots	No.5	I Don't Want To Set The World On Fire
Dinah Shore	No.6	Yes My Darling Daughter
Bing Crosby	No.7	You Are My Sunshine
Hal Kemp & His Orchestra	No.8	So You're The One
The Andrews Sisters	No.9	I'll Be With You In Apple Blossom Time
Vera Lynn	No.10	Over The Hill

N.B. During this era music was dominated by a number of 'Big Bands' and songs could be attributed to the band leader, the band name, the lead singer or a combination of these. On top of this the success of a song was tied to the sales of sheet music, so a popular song would often be perfomed by many different combinations of singers and bands, and the contemporary charts would list the song without clarifying whose version was the major hit. With this in mind although the above chart has been compiled with best intent it does remain subjective.

Glenn Miller & His Orchestra
Chattanooga Choo Choo

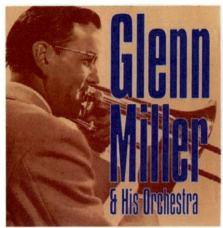 

Label:	Written by:	Length:
HMV	Warren / Gordon	3 mins 31 secs

Alton Glenn Miller (b. 1st March 1904 - MIA 15th December 1944) was a big-band musician, arranger, composer and bandleader in the swing era. He was the best-selling recording artist from 1939 to 1943, leading one of the best-known big bands and scoring 23 No.1 hits. "Chattanooga Choo Choo" featured in the film Sun Valley Serenade (1941) and was the first song to receive a gold record in the U.S.

The Ink Spots
We Three (My Echo, My Shadow & Me)

Label:	Written by:	Length:
Brunswick	Robertson / Cogane / Mysels	3 mins 18 secs

The Ink Spots, Bill Kenny (b. 12th June 1914 - d. 23rd March 1978), Deek Watson (b. 18th July 1909 - d. 4th November 1969), Charlie Fuqua (b. 20th October 1910 - d. 21st December 1971), and Hoppy Jones (b. 17th February 1905 - d. 18th October 1944), were a pop vocal group who gained international fame in the 1930s and 1940s.

Jimmy Dorsey
Maria Elena

Label:	Written by:	Length:
Decca	Barcelata / Russell	3 mins 1 sec

James Francis Dorsey (b. 29th February 1904 - d. 12th June 1957) was a jazz clarinettist, saxophonist, composer and big band leader known professionally as Jimmy Dorsey. He was inducted into the Big Band Hall of Fame in 1983 and is considered one of the most important and influential alto saxophone players of the Big Band and Swing era. Dorsey notably played clarinet on the seminal jazz standards Singin' the Blues (1927) and the original recording of Georgia on My Mind (1930), both of which were inducted into the Grammy Hall of Fame.

Bing Crosby
Dolores

Label:	Written by:	Length:
Brunswick	Alter / Loesser	3 mins 15 secs

Harry Lillis 'Bing' Crosby, Jr. (b. 3rd May 1903 - d. 14th October 1977) was a singer, comedian and an Oscar winning actor who also bred racehorses and co-owned the Pittsburgh Pirates baseball team. Crosby's trademark warm bass-baritone voice made him the best-selling recording artist of the 20th century, selling close to a billion records, tapes, compact discs and digital downloads worldwide.

5. The Ink Spots
I Don't Want To Set The World On Fire

Label:	Written by:	Length:
Brunswick	Benjamin / Marcus / Durham / Seiler	2 mins 48 secs

The Ink Spots were widely accepted in both the white and black communities largely due to the ballad style introduced to the group by lead singer Bill Kenny. Since they disbanded in 1954 there have been well over 100 vocal groups calling themselves The Ink Spots without any right to the name. The original members of the group were inducted into the Rock and Roll Hall of Fame in 1989, and the Vocal Group Hall of Fame in 1999.

Dinah Shore
Yes My Darling Daughter

Label:	Written by:	Length:
Regal Zonophone	Jack Lawrence	2 mins 19 secs

Dinah Shore (b. Frances Rose Shore; 29th February 1916 - d. 24th February 1994) was a singer, actress, television personality and the top-charting female vocalist during the Big Band era of the 1940s and 1950s. After failing singing auditions for the bands of Benny Goodman, and both Jimmy Dorsey and his brother Tommy Dorsey, Shore struck out on her own and became the first singer of her era to achieve huge solo success.

⚫7 Bing Crosby
You Are My Sunshine

Label:	Written by:	Length:
Brunswick	Davis / Mitchell	2 mins 35 secs

Bing Crosby was the first real multimedia star and was a leader in record sales, radio ratings, and motion picture grosses from 1931 to 1954. His early career coincided with recording innovations that allowed him to develop an intimate singing style that influenced many male singers who followed him including Perry Como, Frank Sinatra, Dick Haymes, and Dean Martin. For his achievements Crosby has been recognised with three stars on the Hollywood Walk of Fame; for motion pictures, radio, and audio recording.

⚫8 Hal Kemp & His Orchestra
So You're The One

Label:	Written by:	Length:
HMV	Zaret / Whitney / Kramer	2 mins 48 secs

James Hal Kemp (b. 27th March 1904 - d. 21st December 1940) was a jazz alto saxophonist, clarinettist, bandleader, composer and arranger who was inducted into the Big Band and Jazz Hall of Fame in 1992. "So You're The One" featured a vocal refrain from the big-band singer **Janet Blair** (b. Martha Janet Lafferty; 23rd April 23, 1921 - d. 19th February 19, 2007) who went on to become a popular American film and television actress.

The Andrews Sisters
I'll Be With You In Apple Blossom Time

Label:	Written by:	Length:
Capitol	Tilzer / Fleeson	2 mins 58 secs

The Andrews Sisters were a close harmony singing group from the eras of swing and boogie-woogie. The group consisted of three sisters: LaVerne Sophia (b. 6th July 1911 - d. 8th May 1967), Maxene Angelyn (b. 3rd January 1916 - d. 21st October 1995) and Patricia Marie (b. 16th February 1918 - d. 30th January 2013). Throughout their long career the sisters sold well over 75 million records.

Vera Lynn
Over The Hill

Label:	Written by:	Length:
Decca	Mason	3 mins 24 secs

Dame **Vera Margaret Lynn**, CH DBE OStJ (née Welch; b. 20th March 1917) is a singer, songwriter and actress whose musical recordings and performances were enormously popular during the Second World War. Widely known as the Forces' Sweetheart, during the war she toured Egypt, India and Burma as part of ENSA, giving outdoor concerts for the troops. Lynn is the oldest person to have a No.1 album in the charts (aged 97), and became the first centenarian to have a charting album in 2017 with "Vera Lynn 100".

40

1941: TOP FILMS

1. **How Green Was My Valley** - *20th Century Fox*
2. **Sergeant York** - *Warner Bros.*
3. **The Maltese Falcon** - *Warner Bros.*
4. **The Little Foxes** - *RKO Radio Pictures*
5. **Citizen Kane** - *RKO Radio Pictures*

OSCARS

Best Picture: How Green Was My Valley
Most Nominations: Sergeant York (11)
Most Wins: How Green Was My Valley (5)

Best Director: John Ford - *How Green Was My Valley*

Best Actor: Gary Cooper - *Sergeant York*
Best Actress: Joan Fontaine - *Suspicion*
Best Supporting Actor: Donald Crisp - *How Green Was My Valley*
Best Supporting Actress: Mary Astor - *The Great Lie*

The 14th Academy Awards, honouring the best in film for 1941, were presented on the 26th February 1942 at the Biltmore Hotel in Los Angeles, California.

HOW GREEN WAS MY VALLEY

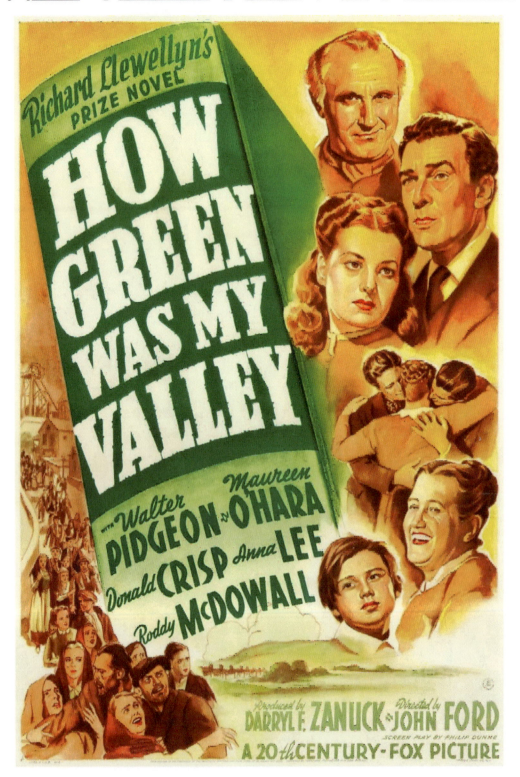

Directed by: John Ford - Runtime: 1h 58min

The story of the Morgans, a hard-working Welsh mining family during the late Victorian era, from the point of view of the youngest child Huw.

Starring

Walter Pidgeon
b. 23rd September 1897
d. 25th September 1984
Character:
Mr. Gruffydd

Maureen O'Hara
b. 17th August 1920
d. 24th October 2015
Character:
Angharad Morgan

Donald Crisp
b. 27th July 1882
d. 25th May 1974
Character:
Gwilym Morgan

Trivia

Interesting Facts | For this film John Ford received his third Academy Award for Best Director, having previously won for The Informer (1935) and The Grapes of Wrath (1940). Eleven years later he would win his fourth for The Quiet Man (1952) (which also starred Maureen O'Hara), a record unmatched by any other director.

It took $110,000 and 150 builders six months to construct Richard Day's elaborate set design on an 80-acre plot in Brent's Crags, near Malibu. The studio brought in blocks of coal weighing over a ton apiece for the construction of the mines and, to create the impression that coal slag covered the landscape in the opening and closing scenes, John Ford had the hillside painted black.

Roddy McDowall had only been in America for two weeks before being cast in the role of Huw. He had been evacuated from Great Britain with his mother and sister to avoid Nazi wartime bombardments.

Although Alfred Newman's justifiably highly-praised score utilised many Welsh melodies as well as the services of virtually every Welsh singer then living in Southern California, his principle love theme was based on the traditional Irish folk song "The Sixpence".

Maureen O'Hara, who was 19 years old at the time of filming, was the film's last surviving cast member at the time of her death (aged 95) in 2015.

Quote | **Huw Morgan**: *[narrating]* Memory... Strange that the mind will forget so much of what only this moment has passed, and yet hold clear and bright the memory of what happened years ago; of men and women long since dead.

SERGEANT YORK

Directed by: Howard Hawks - Runtime: 2h 14min

A marksman is drafted in World War I and ends up becoming one of the most celebrated war heroes.

Starring

Gary Cooper
b. 7th May 1901
d. 13th May 1961
Character:
Alvin C. York

Walter Brennan
b. 25th July 1894
d. 21st September 1974
Character:
Pastor Rosier Pile

Joan Leslie
b. 26th January 1925
d. 12th October 2015
Character:
Gracie Williams

Trivia

Interesting Facts

When informed that Hollywood wanted to make a film about his exploits in World War I, Alvin C. York insisted that only Gary Cooper could play him. At almost 40 years of age Cooper was actually too old to play York - who was not quite 30 at the time of the battle - and York was informed of this, but he insisted that if Cooper couldn't play him, he would not allow the film to be made.

Sergeant York was first film to earn at least 10 Academy Award nominations and not win Best Picture; it won two Academy Awards, Best Actor - Gary Cooper, and Best Film Editing - William Holmes.

In 2008, Sergeant York was selected for preservation in the United States National Film Registry by the Library of Congress as being "culturally, historically, or aesthetically significant".

Alvin C. York himself was on the set for a few days during filming. When one of the crew members tactlessly asked him how many "Jerries" he had killed, York started sobbing so vehemently he threw up. The crew member was nearly fired but the next day York demanded that he keep his job.

This film earned legendary director Howard Hawks his only Best Director Oscar nomination.

Quote

'Pusher' Ross: An' you haven't even seen a subway?
Alvin: I ain't never even heerd o' one.
'Pusher' Ross: 'Heerd'? 'heerd' What kind o' talk is that? Do they all talk that kind of English where you come from?
Alvin: Well there ain't any English people down our way - just Americans.

THE MALTESE FALCON

Directed by: John Huston - Runtime: 1h 40min

San Francisco private eye Sam Spade takes on a case that involves him with three unscrupulous adventurers and their quest for a jewel-encrusted statuette.

Starring

Humphrey Bogart
b. 25th December 1899
d. 14th January 1957
Character:
Samuel Spade

Mary Astor
b. 3rd May 1906
d. 25th September 1987
Character:
Brigid O'Shaughnessy

Gladys George
b. 13th September 1904
d. 8th December 1954
Character:
Iva Archer

Trivia

Goof | *[at around 1h 6min]* "L.A.F.D." (Los Angeles Fire Department) appears on the firefighters' helmets, the film is set in San Francisco.

Interesting Facts | Warner Bros. planned to change the name of the film to "The Gent from Frisco" because the novel's title had already been used for The Maltese Falcon (1931). The studio eventually agreed to keep the original title at John Huston's insistence.

Although he story-boarded every scene, John Huston was open to abandoning his plans if his more experienced cast came up with something better. He estimated that three-quarters of the time he used his original set-ups, but for the remaining quarter he adopted ideas that the cast had come up with.

Humphrey Bogart had to supply his own wardrobe for the film. This was common practice at Warner Brothers as a way for the studio to save money.

Steve Wynn, the Las Vegas hotel and casino billionaire, paid $4.1 million at auction in 2013 for a statuette of the Maltese Falcon from the film. This makes it one of the most valuable film props ever made, costing more than ten times the films original budget.

Quote | **Brigid O'Shaughnessy**: Mr. Archer was so alive yesterday, so solid and hearty...
Sam Spade: Stop it. He knew what he was doing. Those are the chances we take.
Brigid O'Shaughnessy: Was he married?
Sam Spade: Yeah, with ten thousand insurance, no children, and a wife that didn't like him.

THE LITTLE FOXES

Directed by: William Wyler - Runtime: 1h 56min

The ruthless moneyed Hubbard clan lives in, and poisons, their part of the deep South at the turn of the twentieth century.

Starring

Bette Davis
b. 5th April 1908
d. 6th October 1989
Character:
Regina Giddens

Herbert Marshall
b. 23rd May 1890
d. 22nd January 1966
Character:
Horace Giddens

Teresa Wright
b. 27th October 1918
d. 6th March 2005
Character:
Alexandra Giddens

Trivia

Interesting Facts

When the film opened at Radio City Music Hall in New York it set an all-time attendance record for a normal opening day with over 22,000 people attending.

According to Samuel Goldwyn Jr., the reason Jack L. Warner loaned Bette Davis to RKO for this film was to settle a $300,000 gambling debt Warner had with Samuel Goldwyn.

Bette Davis had legendary make-up artist Perc Westmore devise a white mask-like effect for her face to emphasise Regina's coldness. Director William Wyler hated it, likening it to a Kabuki mask.

David Hewitt, the character played by Richard Carlson, does not appear at all in the play. He was added to provide a love interest for Alexandra Giddens (Teresa Wright), and to add another sympathetic male character to the film besides Horace Giddens (Herbert Marshall).

The film features Patricia Collinge's (Birdie Hubbard) only Oscar nominated performance.

Quotes

David Hewitt: You know, that's the first time I ever heard your mother tell you to do something, and you didn't hop to do it.
Alexandra Giddens: That's a funny thing to say.
David Hewitt: You know, you take one step. And then you take another. After a while you'll find out you're walking all by yourself.

David Hewitt: Do you like me?
Alexandra Giddens: Not today.
David Hewitt: Why, I'll come back tomorrow.

CITIZEN KANE

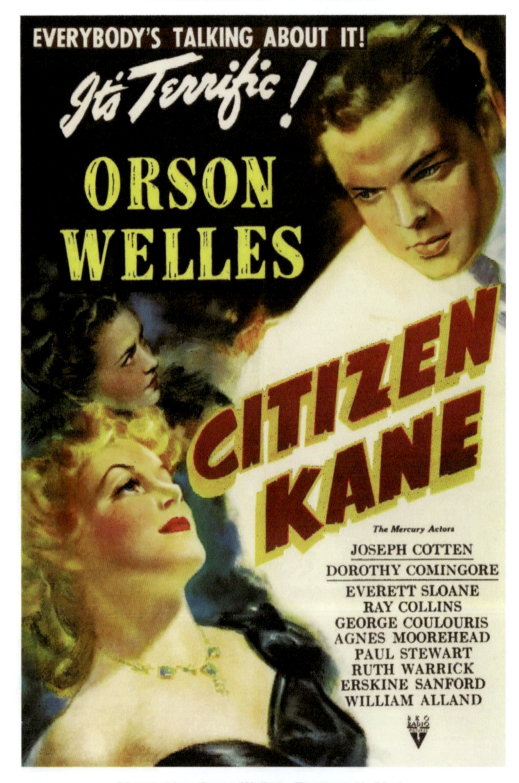

Directed by: Orson Welles - Runtime: 1h 59min

Following the death of publishing tycoon Charles Foster Kane, reporters scramble to uncover the meaning of his final word, "Rosebud".

Starring

Orson Welles
b. 6th May 1915
d. 10th October 1985
Character:
Charles Foster Kane

Joseph Cotten
b. 15th May 1905
d. 6th February 1994
Character:
Jedediah Leland

Dorothy Comingore
b. 24th August 1913
d. 30th December 1971
Character:
Susan Alexander Kane

Trivia

Goof — When Susan Alexander Kane tells Kane that she's leaving him once and for all Kane has a moustache. A second later as he watches her walk away the moustache is gone.

Interesting Facts — To keep studio execs off his back, Orson Welles claimed the cast and crew were "in rehearsal" during the first few days of shooting, when in fact they were actually shooting the film. It took a number of days before the studio caught on.

The film's opening - just the title, no star names - was almost unprecedented in 1941. It is now the industry norm for Hollywood blockbusters.

For this film Orson Welles, along with cinematographer Gregg Toland, pioneered "deep focus", a technique that keeps every object in the foreground, centre and background in simultaneous focus. This brought a sense of depth to the two-dimensional world of movies.

Orson Welles' 156-page personal working copy of the script from the film sold for $97,000 in 2007.

Despite all the publicity the film was a box-office flop and was quickly consigned to the RKO vaults. At 1941's Academy Awards it was booed every time one of its nine nominations were announced. In 1998 The American Film Institute's poll ranked the film No.1 on its list of greatest American movies of all time, and No.1 again on its 10th anniversary in 2007.

Quote — **Charles Foster Kane**: Hello, Jedediah.
Jedediah Leland: Hello, Charlie. I didn't know we were speaking...
Charles Foster Kane: Sure, we're speaking, Jedediah: you're fired.

Sporting Winners

Football

Between 1939 and 1946 normal competitive football was suspended in England and Scotland. Many footballers signed up to fight in the war and as a result many teams were depleted and fielded guest players instead. Appearances in these tournaments did not count in players' official records.

England: The 1940-1941 season was the second season of special wartime football in England. League competition was split into two regional leagues, one North and one South. Teams played as many fixtures as was feasible and winners were decided on goal average rather than points.

Competition	Winner
North Regional League	**Preston North End**
South Regional League	**Crystal Palace**
Football League War Cup	**Preston North End**
London War Cup	**Reading**
Lancashire War Cup	**Manchester United**

Scotland: The 1940-1941 season was the second season of special wartime football in Scotland. The Scottish Football League and Scottish Cup were suspended and in their place regional league competitions were set up.

Competition	Winner
Southern League	**Rangers**
Glasgow Cup	**Celtic**
Southern League Cup	**Rangers**
Summer Cup	**Hibernian**
Renfrewshire Cup	**St Mirren**

International matches: Six unofficial international football games were played in 1941 between England, Scotland and Wales. During this period no caps were awarded.

Date	Result	Date	Result
8/2/1941	England 2-3 Scotland	7/6/1941	Wales 2-3 England
26/4/1941	England 4-1 Wales	4/10/1941	England 2-0 Scotland
3/5/1941	Scotland 1-3 England	25/10/1941	England 2-1 Wales

Rugby - Home Nations

The 1941 Home Nations Championship series was not contested due to the war. International rugby was put on hold and would not resume again until 1947, when the Home Nations would become the Five Nations with the addition of France to the line-up.

Grand National

Although the Grand National was run as normal in 1940 and most other major horse races around the world were able to be held throughout the war, the commandeering of Aintree for defence use in 1941 meant no Grand National could be held between 1941 and 1945.

Epsom Derby - Owen Tudor

The 1941 'New Derby' two furlongs from home; the winner Owen Tudor is far on the right.

Winner.	Jockey	Trainer	Owner	Time
Owen Tudor	**Billy Nevett**	**Fred Darling**	**C. Macdonald-Buchanan**	**2m 32s**

The Derby Stakes is Britain's richest horse race and the most prestigious of the country's five Classics. First run in 1780 this Group 1 flat horse race is open to three year old thoroughbred colts and fillies. Although the race usually takes place at Epsom Downs in Surrey, during both World Wars the venue was changed and the Derby was run at Newmarket; these races are known as the New Derby. *Note: Epsom Downs racecourse was used throughout the war for an anti-aircraft battery.*

Golf - Open Championship

The Open Championship was cancelled in 1941 due to the war and the tournament was not contested again until 1946.

Tennis - Wimbledon

The 1941 Wimbledon Championships was another sporting event cancelled due to World War 2. Hosted since 1877 by the All England Lawn Tennis and Croquet Club in Wimbledon, London, the competition did resume again until 1946.

County Cricket

All first-class cricket was cancelled during the Second World War; no first-class matches were played in England after Friday, 1st September 1939 until Saturday, 19th May 1945.

World Snooker Championship

The World Snooker Championship was cancelled because of the war and was not be held again until 1946.

THE COST OF LIVING

SAVE
FOR NATIONAL SAFETY

DEPOSITS IN TRUSTEE SAVINGS BANKS

help to pay for the cost of the war

ORDINARY ACCOUNTS $2\frac{1}{2}\%$ per annum

INVESTMENT ACCOUNTS $2\frac{3}{4}\%$ per annum

COMPOUND INTEREST

allowed without deductions.
Under direct Government Supervision
and control.

YOUR TRUSTEE SAVINGS BANK

Comparison Chart

	1941	1941 (+ Inflation)	2020	% Change
3 Bedroom House	£800	£45,084	£234,853	+420.9%
Weekly Income	£2.17s.10d	£162.96	£619	+279.8%
Pint Of Beer	9d	£2.11	£3.79	+79.6%
Cheese (lb)	1s.6d	£4.23	£2.98	-29.6%
Bacon (lb)	1s.10d	£5.17	£2.94	-43.1%
The Beano	2d	47p	£2.75	+485.1%

SHOPPING

Brooke Bond Beef Cubes (each)	1d
Rowntree's Cocoa (¼lb)	5d
Bournville Cocoa (¼lb)	5d
Cadbury's Bourn-Vita (½lb)	1s.5d
Plain York Chocolate (¼lb block)	4d
Bassett's Liquorice Allsorts (½lb carton)	10d
Amami Wave Sets	7½d
Eve Shampoo	3d
Lux Toilet Soap (tablet)	4d
Lifebuoy Toilet Soap (tablet)	3d
Gillette Razor Blades (3)	1s.3d
Halex Toothbrush	1s
Kolynos Toothpaste	7½d
Phillips' Dental Magnesia	7½d
Pepsodent Irium Dentifrice	7½d
Milk Of Magnesia Tablets	7d
Rennies (25)	7d
Andrews Liver Salt	10½d
Crookes' Halibut Liver Oil (25 capsules)	2s.6d
Ex-Lax Constipation Relief	2½d
Dr Cassells Nerve Tablets	3s.5d
Beechams Lung Syrup (bottle)	1s.4d
Doans Backache Kidney Pills	1s.5d
Germolene Antiseptic Ointment	7d
Germoplast First Aid Adhesive Plaster (tin)	6d
Cro Pax Corn Caps	9d
Sunlight Washing Flakes	6d
George Bell's Cat Powder (10)	7d
Tibs Cat Tonic (9)	7d

By Appointment to H.M. The King

Feel its TONIC ACTION

You can actually feel Pears Soap doing your skin good while you are washing. A pleasant tingling sensation tells you that its special tonic properties are reviving the vitality which is the secret of a healthy complexion. Pears Soap wears down without waste to the thinnest wafer, and is the most economical of all good toilet soaps.

Pears

TRANSPARENT SOAP   **6**$^{D.}$ **A CAKE**

MATCHLESS FOR THE COMPLEXION

TP 238/19

CLOTHES

Women's Clothing

Samuel Soden Marmot Wallaby Fur Coat	23gns
J. A. Davis & Co Woollen Coat	£5.5s
Schofields Spring Felt Hat	19s.3d
C&A Junior Miss Dress (5 coupons)	19s.11d
Barkers Utility Stockings	2s
Suedette Perforated Court Shoe	8s.11d
Glace Court Slippers	5s.11d

Men's Clothing

Austin Reed Great Coat	10gns
Man's Finest Cloth Suit	5gns
Wilson Brothers Busmen's Suit	£1.12s.6d
Army Boots	10s.6d

The best HOME DEFENCE against dull cooking is BOVRIL

Bovril stimulates the digestive process on which vitality and health depend. It enables you to get full benefit from your food. Bovril makes meals much nicer, as well as more nourishing.

GRANT'S *Scotch* WHISKY

Aged · Of Rare Mellowness · Subtle Bouquet ·

BY HOST · BY GUEST · BY ALL PREFERRED!

Smoke

GREYS CIGARETTES

Just honest-to-goodness pre-war tobacco

10 FOR 9ᴰ   Plain (Green Label) or Cork-tipped (Red Label)

BEER IS BEST! AT ALL ROYAL BREWERY HOUSES
Fight Winter Chills With
BURTON
An Excellent Beer
BEER is BEST
SUPPORT YOUR LOCAL RED CROSS FUND

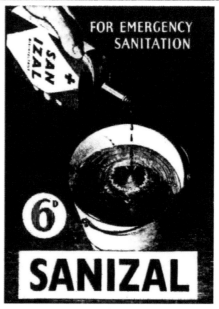

FOR EMERGENCY SANITATION
6ᴰ SANIZAL

OTHER PRICES

HMV 10in Record	2s.5½d
Suit Dry Cleaning & Tailor Pressing	1s.9d
Osbaldiston's Ladies Shopping Bag	3s.6d
Gents Hide Leather Dressing Case	25s
Ladies Brush Set	10s.6d
Lewis's Ready Mixed Paint (5lb tin)	2s
Nutilis Vegetable Fertilizer (bag)	6d
Gumption Smooth Paste Cleaner	6d
White Grape Australian Wine	5s.6d
King Six Cigar (each)	8d
Player's Digger Flake Tobacco (1oz)	1s.3½d
Capstan Navy Cut Cigarettes (20)	1s.5½d
Woman's Weekly Magazine	3d

TOP PRICE
FOR YOUR
OLD GOLD or SILVER
38/- GIVEN FOR YOUR SOVEREIGNS
BLACKWOOD'S, 43, BRIGGATE, SHIPLEY.

Money Conversion Table

Pounds / Shillings / Pence 'Old Money'		Decimal Value	Value 2020 (Rounded)
Farthing	¼d	0.1p	6p
Half Penny	½d	0.21p	12p
Penny	1d	0.42p	23p
Threepence	3d	1.25p	70p
Sixpence	6d	2.5p	£1.41
Shilling	1s	5p	£2.82
Florin	2s	10p	£5.64
Half Crown	2s.6d	12.5p	£7.04
Crown	5s	25p	£14.09
Ten Shillings	10s	50p	£28.18
Pound	20s	£1	£56.36
Guinea	21s	£1.05	£59.17
Five Pounds	£5	£5	£281.78
Ten Pounds	£10	£10	£563.55

SMEDLEY'S ENGLISH GROWN Garden Peas

7d, 8½d and 1/1 per tin

ROBINSON'S (DRIFFIELD) LTD.

Family Grocers and Provision Merchants
Tea Blenders and Coffee Specialists

53 Market Place, Driffield.   Phone 37.

DIAMOND ENGAGEMENT RINGS £5, £10 to £180. **WATCHES** WATCH REPAIRS.

JOHN DYSON & SONS 24-26, BRIGGATE LEEDS

We are Buyers of **OLD GOLD** SECOND-HAND JEWELLERY and **DIAMONDS**

THE BATTLE OF THE ATLANTIC

SPADE versus SUBMARINE

WANTED BY EASTER

150 New Allotment Tenants

FOR

150 New Allotments

NOW READY AND WAITING

AT

RED BECK (near Norwood Terrace)
WROSE
NAB WOOD DRIVE
SPRINGSWOOD
MANOR LANE
WEST ROYD (Leeds Road)

RENT FREE THIS YEAR

Tenancy Guaranteed until End of War.

Apply personally, or by letter or postcard :—

TOWN HALL, SHIPLEY (Clerk's Department)

or any member Shipley Home Food Production Corps.

VEGETABLES — VITAMINS — VICTORY

CARTOONS

The New Order changeth, giving place to Newer.

"Blimey! That's what I told him, sir! But he said 'Rubbish! a man's as old as he feels'!"

Coming Down!

"THAT'S NOT HISTORY, MUSSO—THAT'S US!"

Printed in Great Britain
by Amazon